The Palestinian Vill[...] H[...]me

Suad Amiry and Vera Tam[...]

Published for the Trustees of the British Museum by British Museum Publications

Published by British Museum Publications Ltd
46 Bloomsbury Street, London
WC1B 3QQ

British Library Cataloguing in Publication Data
Amiry, Suad
The Palestinian village home.
1. Palestine. Arab villages.
Vernacular houses. Architectural features
1. Title II. Tamari, Vera
728.3'095694

ISBN 0-7141-1599-1

Designed by Roger Davies

Set in Palatino by M & B (Felsted) Ltd.
Printed in Italy by Arti Grafiche Motta.

The Trustees of the British Museum acknowledge with gratitude the generous grant made by the Ancaster Trust towards the publication of this book.

Front cover: Stone houses in Yatta near Hebron, 1967.
Photo: Shelagh Weir

Back cover: Living room in a house in Silwan, 1886.
Watercolour by James Clark RA, Palestine Exploration Fund

This page: The approach to Halhul near Hebron, 1940.
On the right is the shrine of Nabi Yunis.
Photo: Matson Collection, Library of Congress

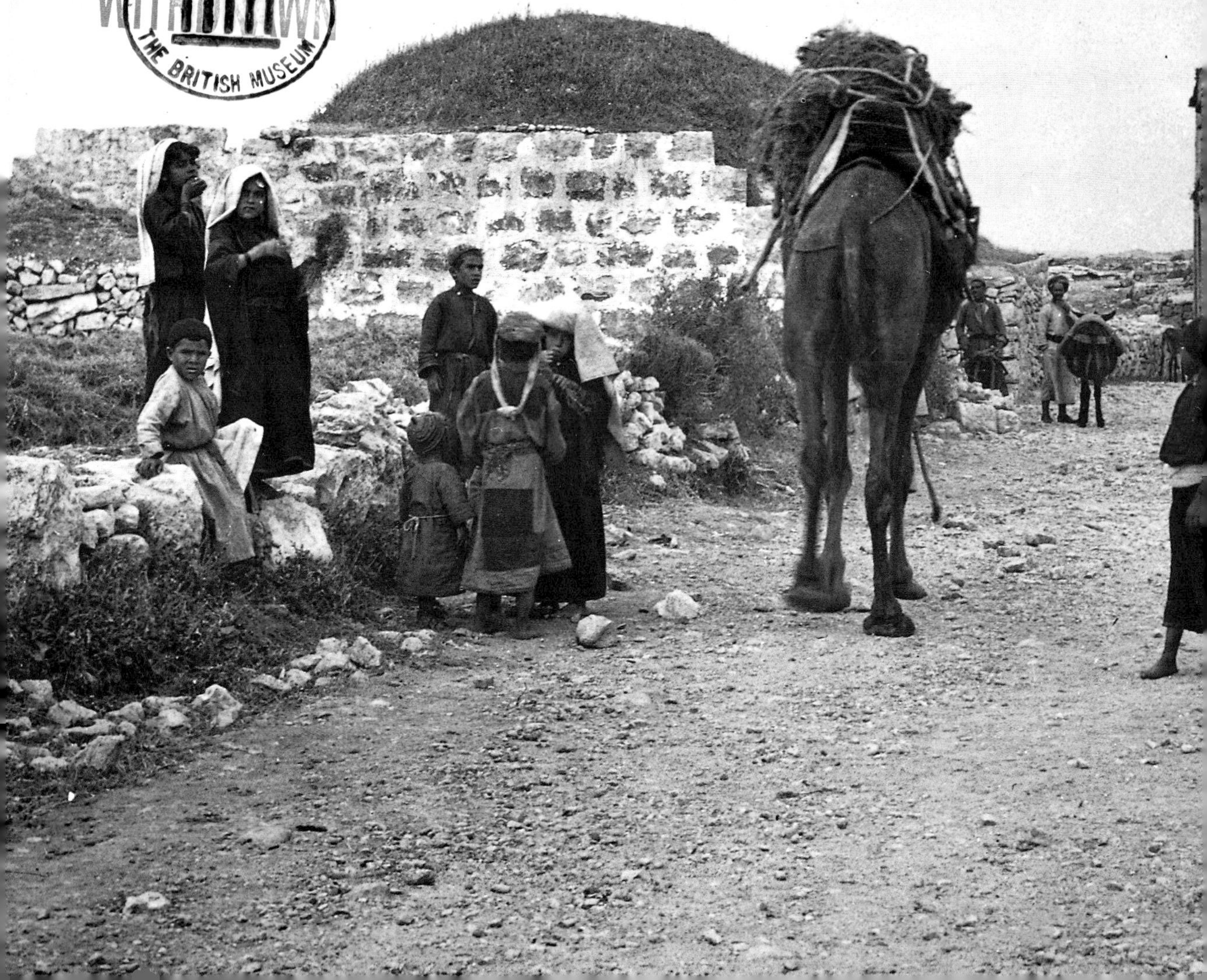

Contents

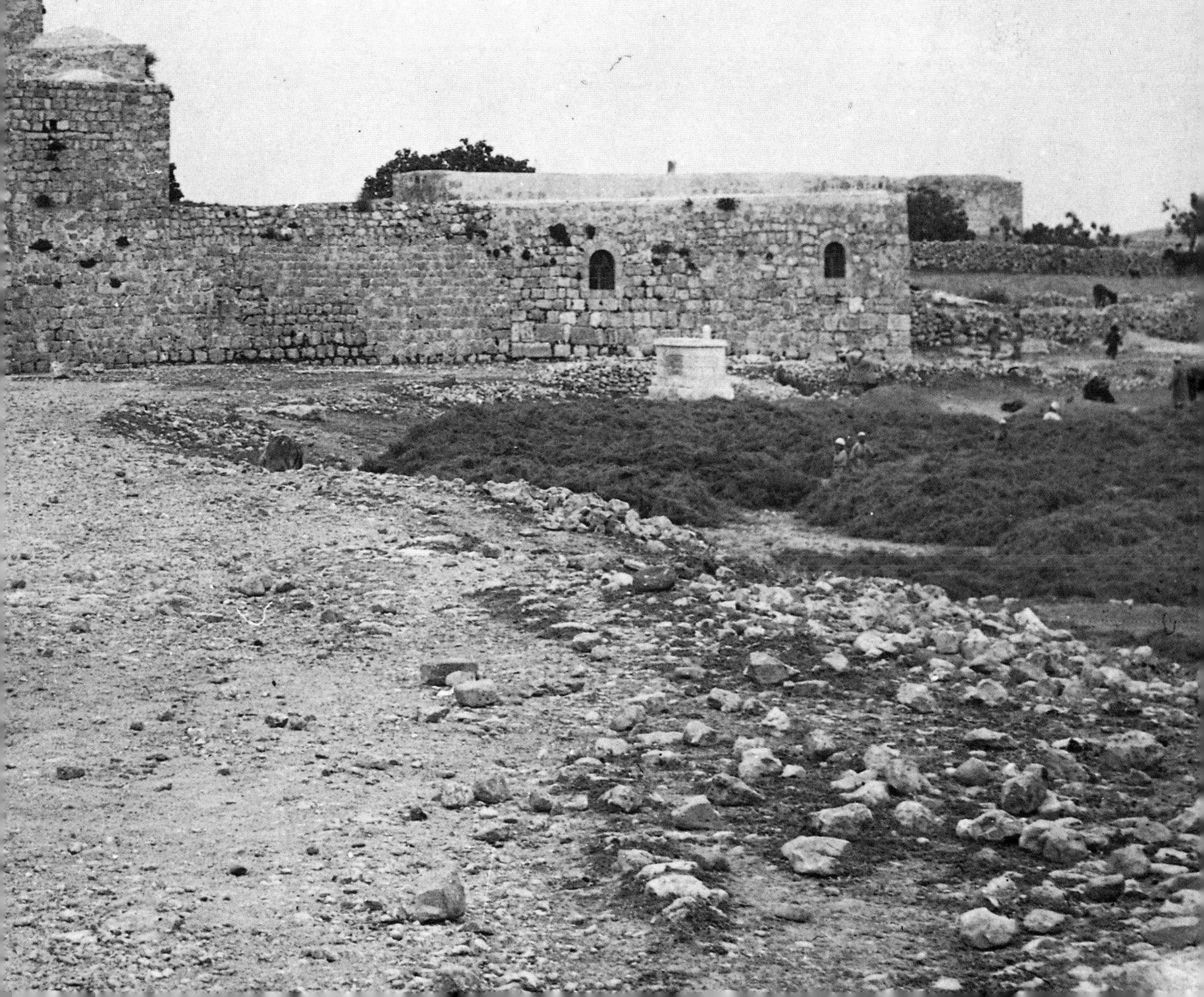

Foreword

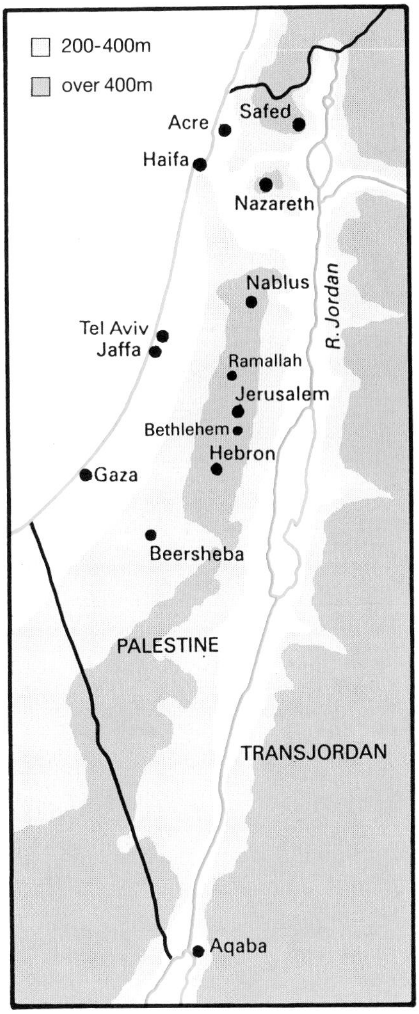

Palestine before 1948, showing main towns and highlands.
Drawn by Rebecca Jewell

The village of Kefr Malik north east of Ramallah, British Mandate period.
Photo: Matson Collection, Library of Congress

Radical transformations have taken place in Palestine since the late nineteenth century which have been reflected in its traditional material culture. This has created an urgent need to document and, where possible, preserve the traditional artefacts and constructions which are rapidly disappearing, and to do this while information about them can still be collected from the generation who remember making and using them. *The Palestinian Village Home* is intended as a contribution to this endeavour, and has been published to coincide with the *Palestinian Costume* exhibition at the Museum of Mankind which opened in late 1989.

This book is concerned with the material culture of the *fellāḥīn*, the village peasants who formed the majority of the Palestinian population, and focuses in particular on the villagers of the central highlands of Palestine at the turn of this century. Most of the information was obtained from field research in the late 1970s and mid 1980s among villagers in the West Bank, and from the study of surviving buildings and artefacts. The illustrations include field photographs taken during this work, archive photographs from the British Mandate period in Palestine (1922-48), and watercolours from the 1880s by James Clark RA. An inspiring reference work has been the photographs taken in the village of Artas, south of Bethlehem, by anthropologist Hilma Granqvist in the 1920s, and published in *Portrait of a Palestinian Village* (K. Seger, 1981). We are grateful to the Library of Congress and the Palestine Exploration Fund for permission to reproduce these pictures.

We are indebted to a number of people for their help in the production of this book. First and foremost we wish to acknowledge the generous assistance of the many villagers who shared their life experiences with us so that we could in turn share them with others. We would especially like to thank Khader and his mother Umm Khader of Qatannah, Umm Elias Khalaf in Ramallah, Umm il-'Abid in Deir al-Sudan, Abu Maher in Al-Bireh, Abu Hani from Deir Ghassaneh, Umm Musa from Sinjil and Umm Nasir and Umm Muhammad from Samu'ah.

Lisa Taraki gave generously of her time in editing and offering insightful remarks on the manuscript. Shelagh Weir proposed and discussed the idea of the book with us, helped select photographs and prepared it for publication. To both of them goes our special gratitude.

We would also like to thank Salim Tamari for his valuable

Terraces in Wadi Battir, central Palestinian highlands, before 1892. On the left is the Jaffa-Jerusalem railway which was built in the late 1880s.
Photo: Krikorian, Palestine Exploration Fund

help in selecting the photographs, Roger Davies for designing the book, the British Museum Photographic Service for studio photographs, and British Museum Publications Limited for agreeing to publish the book.

Introduction

The visitor to a Palestinian village today is struck by the sharp contrast between old and new. At the centre of the village are clusters of old, soft-coloured, traditional houses, their gentle domes blending naturally with the rolling hills surrounding them. Scattered around this old village core are large, individual houses, recently built from smoothly-cut limestone blocks. These modern structures are cluttered by showy multi-faceted walls built in a haphazard order, their flat roofs often crowned by television antennae resembling the Eiffel Tower, symbols of new affluence. Neither the building style nor the 'aesthetics' of these new houses reflect any clear link with the past.

This incongruity in physical appearance and organisation of the modern Palestinian village is due to the social and economic transformations which have greatly affected Palestinian village settlement patterns and daily life since the late nineteenth century. These transformations have come about as a result of the following factors:

(a) the shift in land tenure from communal to private land ownership, begun by the Ottomans in the late nineteenth century, and implemented more thoroughly under the British;

(b) wage labour, which has drawn increasing numbers of villagers away from agriculture. During the British Mandate period, many highland villagers sought employment as labourers in the citrus industry in the coastal plain, or as British Government employees in schools and the police force. The 1950s witnessed another wave of labour migration towards the Arab Gulf and the two Americas; and during the 1970s, large numbers of Palestinian villagers found employment in Israeli farms, factories, construction projects and the service sector.

These factors contributed towards the marginalisation of agriculture, the fragmentation of extended family landholdings, and the trend towards the nucleation of the family. The accumulation of wealth from wage labour also contributed to the great changes which took place in the material aspects of traditional village life. These changes are manifested most prominently in building and construction, where new materials, building techniques and spatial formations are responses to individual needs rather than to the social and spatial rules that formerly determined the shape of traditional Palestinian homes.

The turn of the century was a relatively stable period, especially in the central highlands (known today as the West

Bank) where rural sheikhs enjoyed a quasi-independent status. The coastal plain was subject to much greater political, social and demographic transformations, the most critical of which was brought about by Jewish colonial settlement which started in 1882 (and has continued until today).

Later, the establishment of the State of Israel in 1948 and the devastating dispersion of a large proportion of the Palestinian people was a crucial factor in the decline and disappearance of Palestinian urban and rural settlements on the coastal plain. After 1948 approximately 390 Palestinian Arab villages inside the State of Israel were eradicated, most of them in the plain (Abdulfattah, 1983). The villagers of the central highlands, with whom this book is concerned, were less drastically affected by these events, since they came under Jordanian rule in 1948. They have, however, been greatly affected by the Israeli occupation which began in 1967, and by the economic changes of the past four decades.

Women seated under a brushwood shelter in their courtyard, Yatta near Hebron, 1967. Behind the donkey is the bread oven *(ṭābūn)* made from mud mixed with straw.
Photo: Shelagh Weir

The village of Yatta south of Hebron, mid 1980s. Note how closely the houses are clustered together.
Photo: Suad Amiry

The Village

Most villages in the central highlands of Palestine are located on hilltops or the upper slopes of the hills overlooking the valleys and plains below, and blending naturally into the surrounding rocky landscape. The compact groups of old houses in greying limestone merge harmoniously with the stone terraces *(sanāsil)* of fruit gardens and orchards. Only occasionally does the minaret of the mosque change the focus, raising the eye from the domed houses to the open expanse of the bright blue sky.

This was the picturesque setting of a Palestinian village until the 1920s. Each village, a tight cluster of small houses, was separated from others by well-tended private gardens *(hawakir)* and then by fields, where a variety of rain-fed crops – olives, figs, almonds, grapes, vegetables and cereals – were cultivated for home consumption and the market.

This settlement pattern was determined by the scarcity of fertile lands in the hilly regions, the fear of bedouin raids and the land tenure system which did not allow private or public building on the valuable agricultural land in the valleys or plains. The only structures built on the terraces were field storage houses *(quṣūr)*. These square or round buildings of neatly-aligned rubble stones were used to store summer crops and to house the peasant and his family during the summer months when they harvested their crops. Other buildings outside the village were the holy shrines *(maqāmāt)*, which commemorated popular holy men associated with the rituals and beliefs of the villagers.

Today the settlement pattern of Palestinian villages is very different. Neighbouring villages are not as distinctly separated, and the new, fashionable houses are now built away from the village core, and spread along major routes, often linking up with neighbouring villages.

Most highland villages were architecturally quite simple. The more sophisticated central highland villages were known as 'throne villages' *(qurā al-karāsi)*, and were centres of power and prestige for the rural landlords *(shuyūkh al-nawāḥi)* who resided in them. Throne villages borrowed some architectural features and building styles from nearby urban centres, reflecting the close economic and political alliances that existed between rural landlords and urban notables.

The physical and spatial organisation of the village, and its division into private and communal areas, was influenced by status, kinship and gender relations as well as communal and

Overleaf: Women and children at the village spring, Artas, 1979.
Photo: Shelagh Weir

Men gathered outside the guest house, Halhul south of Hebron, 1940. Note the musician playing the pipes on the left.
Photo: Matson Collection, Library of Congress

religious needs. Each village contained a number of patrilineal descent groups *(ḥamūleh)* grouped into separate quarters named after them, *(ḥārāt)*, each housing smaller groups made up of several extended families. Village fields were also divided into kinship domains.

Most villages were also subdivided on the basis of social prominence and wealth. The more influential *ḥamūlehs* inhabited the more elevated areas of the village *(al-ḥārah al-fōqah)*, while those which were less well-endowed resided in the lower quarter *(al-ḥārah al-taḥtah)*.

Other areas in the village accommodated the communal needs of the villagers. The main plaza *(sāḥah)* was a meeting place for the men of the village, since they could not meet in each others' homes because the house was considered 'female territory'. The guest-house *(maḍāfah)*, usually situated in the *sāḥah*, was also the centre of male gatherings and entertainment. During the day, the elders of the village would gather there, and in the evenings, after they had returned from working in the fields, the younger men would meet there, to relax, exchange news and perhaps listen to popular tales or folk songs recited by the village musician *(zajjāl)* strumming his single-stringed fiddle *(rabābeh)*. The village mosque was another important meeting place for men.

While these public areas were dominated by men, other areas were the province of women, principally the village spring *('ayn)*. One of a woman's first duties of the day was to fetch water and bring it back to the home. At the turn of the century, the mother of the family sometimes took her children to the spring and did the family washing – soaking the clothes, laying them out on rocks and pounding them with wood. Soap was rarely available so either breadcrumbs, wood ashes or a special kind of sandy clay was used to rub off the dirt. The spring was also where young children were bathed. The bread oven *(ṭābūn)* was another meeting place for women of the same quarter (see below).

Often two or more *ḥamūlehs* shared ownership of the village oil-presses *(al-badd)*, threshing floors *(al-bayāder)*, and local shops which were centres for the daily activities of the members of the different *ḥamūlehs*.

The House (al-dār)

Members of each *ḥamūleh* lived in a group of adjacent houses connected by one or more courtyards *(ḥōsh)*. The houses were grouped round the courtyards in different ways depending on closeness to the family patriarch, and the family's needs for privacy and seclusion. Sons would move out of the family house after they married and would establish separate domestic units adjacent to those of their fathers', often sharing the same courtyard. Generally, the more distant the relationship in a single *ḥamūleh*, the more pronounced the separation between the houses. Houses of cousins, for instance, were often separated from the main grouping of houses by unpaved pathways or winding narrow alleys. Theoretically, however, the houses still belonged to the same quarter.

The courtyard (ḥōsh)

The *ḥōsh* was a semi-private family compound, and was sometimes defined by a large, arched doorway leading from the alley. The organisation of this open space, and the activities which took place there, reveal the significance of the courtyard in the dynamics of Palestinian family life and the management of daily activities.

The courtyard was where women carried out their daily work and mixed with female relatives or neighbours without inhibition or restriction. It was also an ideal playground for the children. During summer nights, the courtyard became a meeting place for family members as they discussed the affairs of the *ḥamūleh* or their work.

Within each courtyard were several smaller, semi-private areas, each leading to an individual house. These front yards were defined either by steps from the main courtyard, or by low walls of rubble stone. Here, women carried out most of the domestic activities of the household – washing dishes and clothes, preparing food, grinding wheat, gleaning grain or pursuing one of the seasonal village crafts in which they specialised, such as pottery, basketry and making storage bins *(khawābi*, sing. *khābiyeh)* and other kitchen articles from mud and straw. It is also where the main evening meal was taken,

The courtyard of an extended family in Yatta near Hebron. Most of a woman's domestic work takes place in the courtyard.
Photo: Suad Amiry

Facing page, above: Women embroidering in their courtyard, Bethlehem, British Mandate period.
Photo: Matson Collection, Library of Congress

Facing page, below: A mud-walled bower *(m'arrash)* roofed with branches, southern Hebron Hills. Shelters are constructed in this region to provide a shaded area outside the house during the hot summer.
Photo: Suad Amiry

Above: A village family outside their house, 1919. This posed picture contains a number of household artefacts: a water jar *(zīr)*, often placed at the entrance of houses; a basketry bowl covered with hide; a hand mill inside a mud container; a brazier *(qānūn)* and a cradle. British Mandate period.
Photo: Matson Collection, Library of Congress

cooked in a metal or clay pot over a fire of sticks in a round brazier *(qānūn)* made out of mud.

A number of household articles were to be found in these front yards: large clay water-storage jars *(zīr)*, constantly replenished with cold drinking water, vast copper washing tubs, tin can containers, firewood and brush collected by the women of the family, stone grain mills, and containers for fodder and water for livestock. Foodstuffs such as tomatoes, raisins and figs were dried here. The family laundry was draped on clothes lines or on the stone walls, and occasionally, colourful mattresses and bedding were hung outside in the sun for airing.

Artas south of Bethlehem, 1979. On the right is the village mosque, and on the left examples of recent village architecture.
Photo: Shelagh Weir

Facing page: Building a house in the Palestinian highlands, British Mandate period. House-building was a co-operative venture, and involved both men and women.
Photo: Matson Collection, Library of Congress

The bread oven (ṭābūn)

At one end of the courtyard was the quarter's communal bread oven *(ṭābūn)*. This small conical structure was made from stone rubble, and roofed either by a stone vault or wooden beams. Inside, there was a circular mud case, known as 'the house of bread' *(bayt al-'aysh)*, which was placed over a shallow fuel pit. This case was approximately 70-80 cm in diameter at the base, tapering to an open top of about 40 cm, and was built by women from a local yellow clay *(ḥuwwār)* mixed with straw.

The oven was heated by sticks and crushed olive pits. Once the fuel was glowing, it was topped with small, smooth pebbles. The open top of the case was then covered by a tin sheet with a handle, and dried dung and other slow-burning

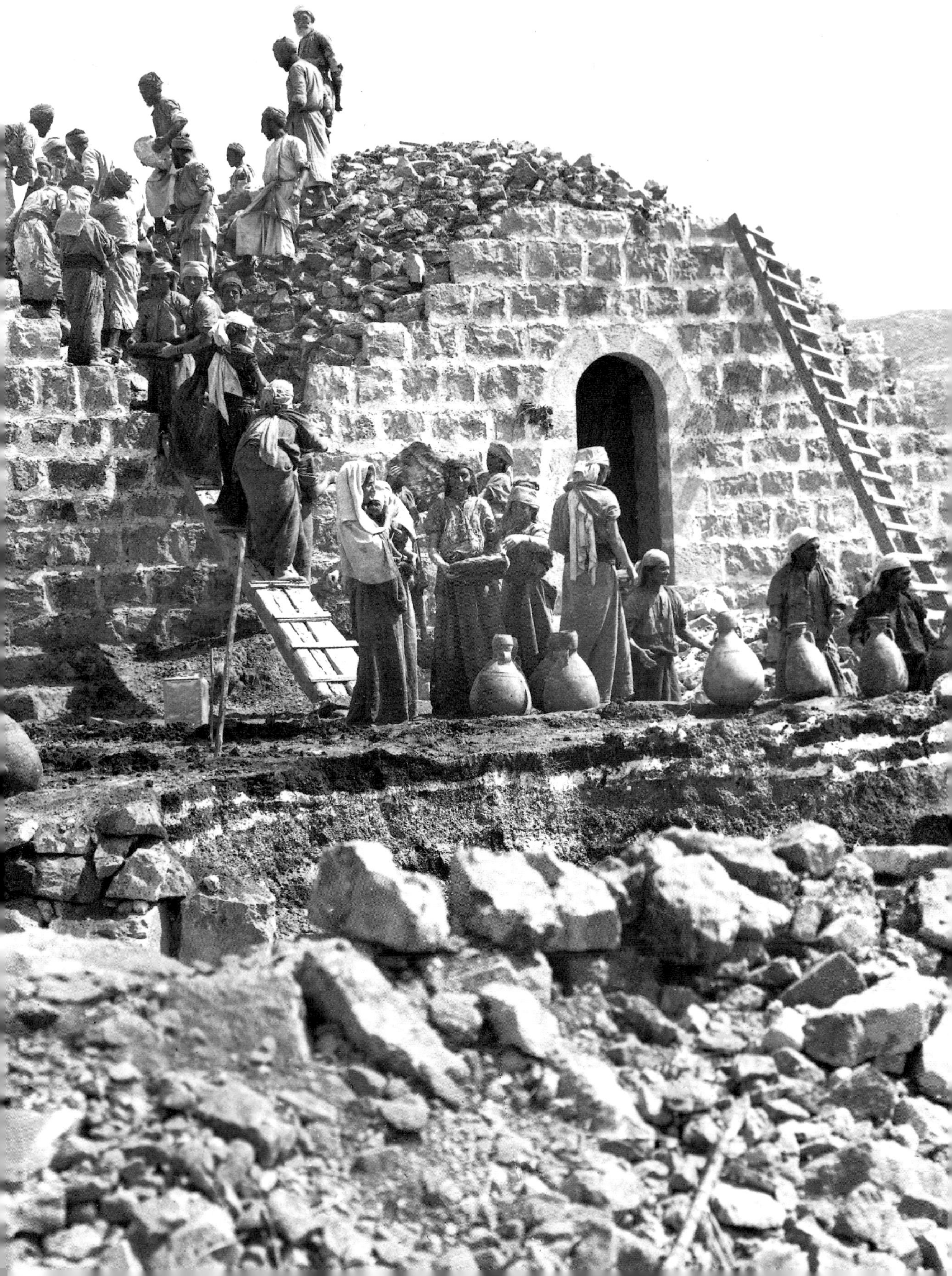

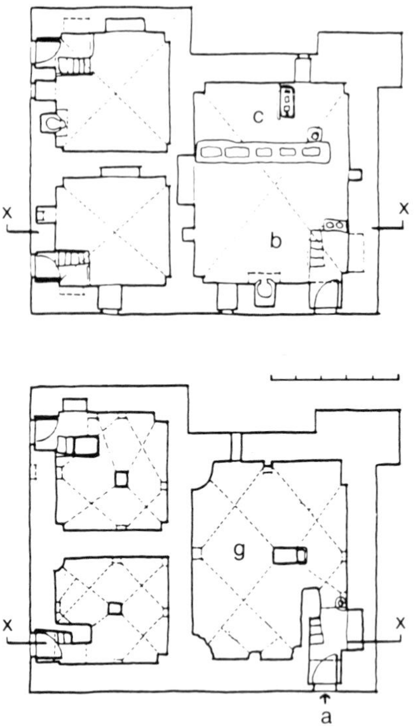

Plan of the house of Abu Helweh in the village of ‘Ebwein near Ramallah. *Above:* upper level; *below:* lower-level *(qā‘ al-bayt).*

a. main entrance
b. family living space *(masṭabeh)*
c. food storage area *(rāwiyeh)*
d. mud-bins *(khawābi)* for food storage and dividing room
e. fireplace *(mawqid)*
f. bedding niche *(qōs)*
g. lower part of the house *(qa‘ al-bayt),* for livestock and agricultural equipment

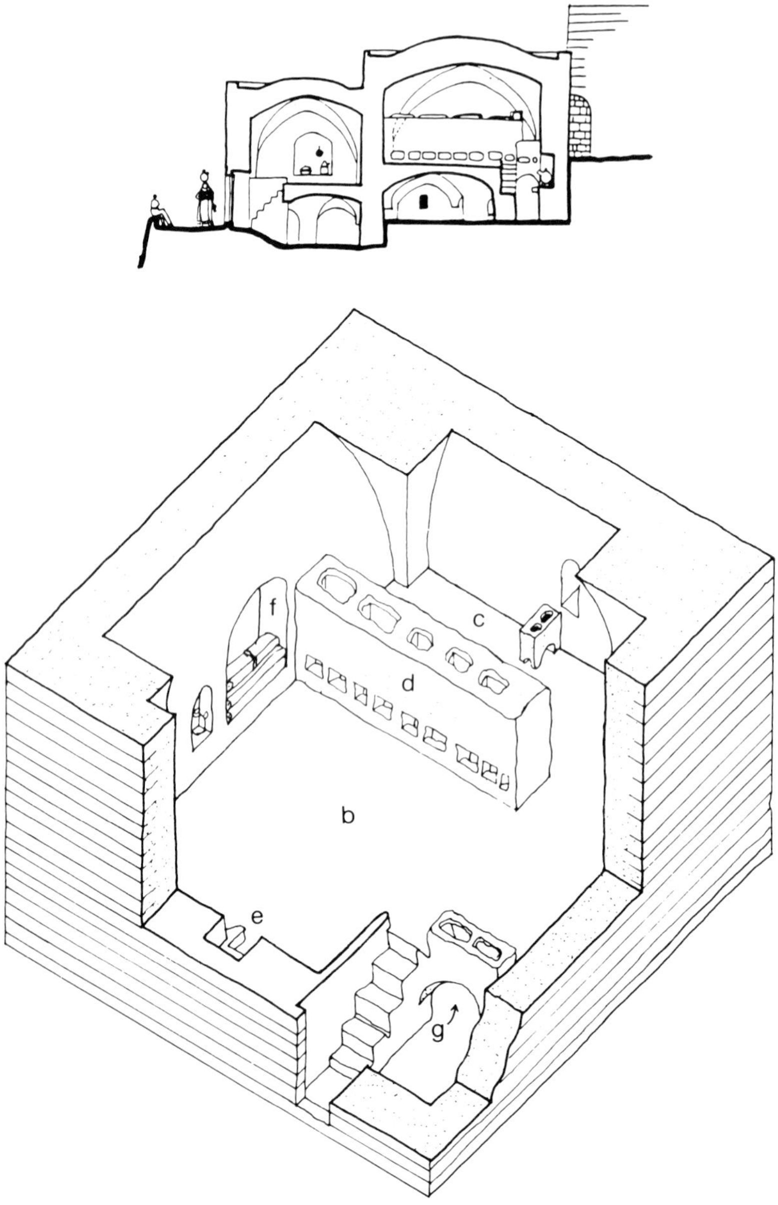

Cross section (through x – x) and isometric diagram of the main living room *(masṭabeh)* of the same house (see key on left).

Facing page, above: Two storey houses in the ‘throne’ village of Ras Karkar near Ramallah, mid 1980s. The big archway leads to a stable *(riwāq).*
Photo: Suad Amiry

Facing page, below: The mansion of Sheikh Sihwail in the ‘throne’ village of ‘Ebwein near Ramallah, mid 1980s.
Photo: Suad Amiry

The village of Al-Janyeh, mid 1980s.
Photo: Suad Amiry

Above: Baking bread in 'Aboud, 1975.
Photo: Shelagh Weir

materials were put around the mud hearth for additional heat. Once the proper temperature was obtained, soft dough cakes were placed over the hot non-stick pebbles and baked.

The *ṭābūn* played an important role for the village women, who would sit inside its cramped interior telling jokes and exchanging news while their bread baked. The *ṭābūn* therefore functioned for women as the guest-house *(maḍāfeh)* did for men.

The façade of the house

Most highland village houses were simple square structures built from the limestone rock abundant in the surrounding hills, and often looked like an extension of nature, with wild plants and shrubs sprouting from cracks between the stones or growing freely on the domed roof. In springtime these plants often bloomed in colourful hanging bouquets of bright pinks and yellows, contrasting beautifully with the grey stone.

Most houses were single-storey, with only one low, arched entrance. In older houses there were no other openings apart from small ventilation holes. However, later houses dating from the Mandate period have relatively large windows, often in pairs (called *mijwiz).* The house walls were massive, sometimes one metre thick, in order to support the heavy stone vault of the roof. Each row of stones *(midmak)* comprised

Above: The main entrance of the mansion of Sheikh Saleh in Deir Ghassaneh near Ramallah, mid 1980s. The finely-dressed white and pink stones, the segmented arch, and the stone seats *(maqsaleh)* flanking the door, are all features copied from Late Mamluk urban architecture.
Photo: Suad Amiry

Above right: An elaborately carved interlocking vousoir in the door arch of the mansion of Sheikh Saleh in Deir Ghassaneh near Ramallah.
Photo: Suad Amiry

an outer and inner layer of stone blocks, with the space between filled with mortar and stone rubble *(dabish)*. This impermeable façade was an effective security measure against robbers.

It was common to whitewash part of the front façade, particularly the arched doorway, since white was a symbol of blessing *(barakeh)*, and gave the appearance of purity and cleanliness. Other touches of colour were the wooden panels of the door painted blue or green. These auspicious colours suggested prosperity and benediction to the owners. For more blessings, the names of God, the Prophet Muhammad, or a cross were inscribed on the keystone of the door alongside other simple carved motifs.

Houses belonging to more prosperous families, especially in 'throne' villages, had urban architectural features such as finely-dressed and decorated stone work, and elaborately carved decorations above doorways and cornices. These were marks of master-builders *(m'allimīn)* hired from nearby urban centres. These wealthier houses often had two or three storeys, and the *'illayeh*, the master bedroom or the guest room on the top floor, symbolised family power and prestige.

The house interior

To enter the house, one had to step over an elevated threshold, *('atabeh),* a symbolic gesture in the passage from the outside world to the intimate privacy of the home. The villager always uttered the name of Allah as he crossed the threshold of his house so as to pacify the *jinn,* which were believed to reside under the *'atabeh.* On first entering her husband's home, a bride had to stick a piece of fermented dough on the door lintel for prosperity and fertility, and it was also considered a good omen if she stepped over the threshold with her right foot first.

House interiors were dark, the only light coming from the single low entrance and the narrow ventilation holes. In summer, when many activities took place in the courtyard outside, the dimly-lit cool interior seemed solemn and orderly, contrasting dramatically with the bright and busy sunny exterior.

The internal arrangement of the one-roomed peasant home projected a model of harmony between the various structural, functional and aesthetic elements. The domed room, approximately 5 × 7 m, was divided into three major areas which met the villagers' social and practical needs: the main family living space *(masṭabeh)* and the food storage space *(rāwiyeh),* both occupying the upper levels, and the *qā 'al-bayt,* at a lower level, for livestock and farming equipment. The organisation of the *masṭabeh* was simple: there were no proper walls separating the different activity areas, and only a series of tall storage bins *(khawābi)* divided the *masṭabeh* from the *rāwiyeh.*

The fireplace *(mawqid* or *wujaq)* was the main focus of the *masṭabeh* and was built of stone along the same wall as the door. The fireplace area was used mostly on cold rainy days when family activities shifted indoors. There the family sat close together trying to warm themselves, as the fireplace was usually the only source of heat in the house. While the women cooked meals in the fireplace, the rest of the family sat around helping or chatting.

On the wall next to the fireplace hung cooking utensils, including wood or metal ladles *(maghārif),* metal sieves *(miṣfāh),* straw trays *(ṭabaq)* and paraffin lamps *(srāj).* The fireplace had an arched opening and was about 120 cm high, 80 cm wide and 40 cm deep. Above it was a shelf on which stood objects such as kettles *(abārīq),* and small pottery jugs. Inside the fireplace, a mud brazier was propped up on a stand 15 cm high, and a two-handled earthen cooking pot *(qidreh)* was used for cooking stew and rice. Around the fireplace were

View inside the living room *(mastabeh)* of a house in Silwan near Jerusalem, 1886. A number of typical household utensils are pictured, including a large water jug *(zīr)*, a circular basketry mat *(ṭabaq)*, a wooden bowl *(bāṭiyeh)*, a floor mat and a hammock cradle.
Watercolour by James Clark RA, Palestine Exploration Fund.

arranged a number of cooking vessels *(ṭanājir)*, an assortment of pottery and wooden bowls, and a large wooden bowl *(bāṭiyeh)*, an important kitchen item, used for kneading dough.

It was at the fireplace that the family took their main, evening meal when the weather was too bad to prepare and eat it outside. The whole family joined together for this meal, which usually consisted of one kind of vegetable cooked with tomato sauce. Either rice, cracked wheat *(burghul)* or lentils were served on the side. Meat was available only once or twice a week, but was always served on festive occasions, such as weddings or circumcisions. The meal was always started by a blessing of the food with the word *bismallāh* (in the name of God). Two large bowls, one of vegetable stew, one of the side dish, were then placed on a straw tray in the middle of the floor with a large number of bread loaves. The whole family squatted round the bowls, sharing out the food and eating with their hands or with spoons. They drank lots of water.

Most village homes contained little furniture – people sat on

View inside the living room *(maṣṭabeh)* of a house in Silwan near Jerusalem, 1886. In the centre and on the left are two mud storage bins *(khawābi)*, and near the entrance are a grain mill, and various bowls and sieves. Bedding is laid out on the floor.
Watercolour by James Clark RA, Palestine Exploration Fund

the floor on closely-woven reed mats *(ḥuṣūr)* on which were placed long flat cotton mattresses *(masānid)* which were moved about as required. Only the richer homes possessed wooden sofas *(dawāshiq)*, wardrobes and beds, imported from the towns.

A cradle, mud storage bins *(khawābi)* and the bridal chest *(ṣandūq al-'arūs)* were the only furniture in the *maṣṭabehs* of most villagers. The bridal chest was a rectangular wooden box carved and painted with colourful floral designs, or studded in a more sophisticated manner with metal nails and flattened metal strips, depending on the wealth and status of the bride's family. This chest was carried from the bride's house at marriage as part of her trousseau, and was her most cherished belonging for it was the only household item which gave her a sense of privacy in the communal space of her in-laws. She alone carried the key to the chest in which she stored her embroidered dresses, shawls and other personal belongings, and even her husband had no right to open it. The position of

the bridal chest in the house defined the area the newly-wed couple would occupy.

Instead of cupboards and shelves, the village house had arched niches *(ṭāqah)* in the walls. These contained objects such as the water pitcher, a lamp and food containers. Sometimes wooden pegs were driven into the wall on which would hang clothes, baskets and other items.

The most important recess was the *qōs* or *mirkaz*, a large, deep, arched recess in which mattresses, blankets and pillows were stored. The opening of the *qōs* was normally covered with a curtain *(jlāleh)* for protection against dust. At the end of the day the bedding was rolled out of the *qōs* and spread on the *masṭabeh* floor for the family to sleep on.

The most important articles of furniture in the house were

Above: House interior, 'Ebwein near Ramallah, mid 1980s. The family's livestock was kept in the lower part of the house *(qā' al-bayt)* (on the right), and the mud storage bin *(khābiyeh)* behind the woman separated the family living room from the food storage area.
Photo: Suad Amiry

Right: Interior of a Ramallah house, British Mandate period. On the right is a bedding store formed from mud against the wall of a tall mud bin *(khābiyeh)*; sieves hang on the wall; and on the left is a brazier *(qānūn)*. The woman on the left is grinding grain on a hand mill. The arches leading to the lower area of the house *(qā' al-bayt)* can be clearly seen below the living area *(masṭabeh)* where the women are sitting.
Photo: American Colony

Women inside their house, Ramallah, 1906. On the right, bedding is stacked in a large, arched wall niche *(qōs)*. The wall is whitewashed and decorated with simple paintings, and the women are seated on a straw mat.
Photo: Standard Scenic Company, Library of Congress

the *khawābi*, the mud bins made by the women for food storage as well as to act as space dividers. Each *khābiyeh* stored a year's supply of wheat, lentils, barley, dried figs *(quṭṭayn)* and raisins *(zbīb)*. The bins consisted of a row of tall, separate units which opened from the top. At the bottom, there was a small opening *(rozanah)*, through which the contents were drawn. The *rozanah* was usually closed by a cloth which, when removed, enabled the food to roll down into a bowl placed beneath it.

Above: A peasant family seated round a brazier *(qānūn)*, an alternative to the fireplace for cooking and heating.
Photo: UNRWA Collection

Facing page: Various basketry articles from the Sinjil area north of Ramallah, 1960s. From left to right: a tray *(ṭabaq)*; a bowl; a wall decoration with a pocket for trinkets; and a trinket box *(qūṭeh)*. The latter two articles are decorated with floss silk.
Museum of Mankind: Q78 AS21 (D.38 cm); 1971 AS2 20 (D.34.5 cm); 1968 AS12 73 (H.46 cm); 1968 AS12 74 (H.40 cm)

Sometimes the *khawābi* were built in the form of a cupboard, and contained shelves or mattress compartments similar to those of the wall niche *(qōs)*.

Women built the *khawābi* in the courtyards with a mixture of red clay *(samqah)*, fine straw particles and water. They were left to dry in the sun, then brought inside by men. Large bins were built up round a supporting framework of poles and reeds *in situ*. Bin surfaces were often whitewashed then decorated with fine reliefs using motifs such as the palm tree, a symbol of life, or the serpent, a symbol of fertility.

The lower level of the houses *(qāʻ al-bayt)* was entered from the main entrance which first led to a small service area before extending into the deeper, darker space where the family livestock (mainly goats, donkeys and chickens) were kept at night. Villagers also stored farming equipment and tools there. Propped against the wall would be a wooden pitchfork *(midhrah)*, the threshing board *(lōḥ al-drās)*, the plough *(miḥrath)*, donkey harnesses and axes. Firewood, dung, barrels, a pail and rope for drawing water from the well *(dalū)*, and rubber containers *(qufaf)* were also stored in this section of the house.

Agriculture and Food Production

The peasant's year was divided into six agricultural seasons *(mawāsim)*. The most important were harvest time *(mawsim al-ḥaṣād)*, the fig and grape season *(mawsim al-ta'zīb)*, and the olive-picking season *(mawsim al-zaytūn)*. The whole family participated in these activities.

Though most agricultural activity was considered to be a male responsibility, women's participation was crucial, particularly during the harvest. The peasant's numerous tasks included ploughing, sowing, planting and pruning trees, threshing and winnowing grain, carrying produce from the fields, repairing tools, building and repairing rubble walls *(sanāsil)*, and house construction.

Harvest time

During the harvest (April-May for barley and June for wheat), the village was almost deserted as most of the inhabitants went down to the fields, leaving older people and a few others behind to guard the property. Before sunrise, members of the

Left: Men winnowing at the threshing floor, Halhul south of Hebron, 1940.
Photo: Matson Collection, Library of Congress

Above: Woman sifting wheat grain with a sieve, Ramallah area, British Mandate period.
Photo: Matson Collection, Library of Congress

family would start gathering the food, tools, animals and other equipment for the harvest, which lasted several days. In the fields, men reaped the crop using sickles, while women and older children gathered the sheaves of wheat and tied them into manageable bundles. Once this was over, the donkeys were loaded with as many bundles as possible, so that often only the head and part of the legs were visible. Women and young girls also carried bundles on their heads as the whole family headed towards the village threshing floor *(baydar).*

The *(baydar)* was owned by the whole village as communal property *(musha')*, and was normally near the village in a location exposed to the wind. In most mountain villages, the threshing floor was a huge flat rock, in the middle of which the sheaves were heaped. Whatever pair of animals was available (mules, donkeys, camels, oxen or horses), they were tied together and driven in circles around the heap, dragging behind them the threshing sledge *(lōḥ al-drās).* This was a thick wooden plank with sharp metal pieces inset beneath, and the friction was increased by one or two persons standing on it as it was driven over the grain. When the wind was favourable, the crushed sheaves were thrown into the air with the winnowing fork to separate them into grain, stalks and straw. The women, sitting on the ground, used variously-sized sieves *(ghurbāl)* to sift the dirt from the grain. After weighing the crop for taxation purposes, the men filled the sacks with grain, tied the stalk bundles *(qash)* for use in basket-making, and gathered the straw *(quswal)* for use as animal fodder, fuel or for mixing with mud for building containers and utensils.

At the end of the day, the animals were loaded with the gathered produce, and the *fellāḥ* with the rest of his family returned home and stored it in the mud bins inside the house.

The olive-picking season (mawsim al-zaytūn)

Olives and olive oil were, and still are, the most valuable produce of the Palestinian countryside, and most village fields contained olive groves. The olive-picking season, which lasted between two and four weeks (depending on the number of olive trees a family owned), began in late October or early November. In most villages, a specific date was set by the village council of elders announcing the beginning of the olive-picking season. Setting such a date was necessary in order to prevent individual peasants from competing with others by marketing their produce earlier. It also deterred villagers from picking their neighbours' olives, since family groves were adjacent to one another and had no clear boundaries.

Facing page: Beating the olives from the trees, highland Palestine, British Mandate period.
Photo: Matson Collection, Library of Congress

Right: Woman crushing olives with a stone, Ramallah area, British Mandate period.
Photo: American Colony, Jerusalem

Early in the morning on the specified day, all the inhabitants of the village went to the olive groves with their mules and donkeys loaded with ladders, baskets, sacks, long sticks and food. Once there the men spread sheets on the ground beneath the trees, climbed the trees or a ladder, and shook the olives down onto the sheets. Alternatively, the branches were beaten with long sticks. Women and children then put the olives in straw baskets which were emptied into large sacks.

The olive season was a festive time for the villagers, and the strenuous labour was often accompanied by songs celebrating the quality of their produce and the collective spirit of their work.

Before dark, the whole family loaded the sacks of olives on

the mules and donkeys and returned to the village. There the olives were first piled up in heaps, then spread out either inside the house, outside in the courtyard, or on the roofs of the houses. They were left for three to four days to reduce the acidity of the olive oil.

Part of the olive harvest was processed for domestic consumption. Big green olives were selected, crushed by a stone, and pickled in brine with pieces of lemon and hot green peppers. Black olives were pickled differently: after being heavily salted, they were put away in sacks or baskets for two to three weeks, when they were soaked in hot boiling water to remove the bitterness; they were then stored in jars filled with water and olive oil.

The bulk of the olive harvest was taken by the men to the village or neighbourhood oil press *(badd)*. This consisted of two huge circular stones, the upper of which was generally turned by a mule, donkey or horse, pressing the olives underneath; the oil flowed into a channel and was collected in jars. The residue of olives was pressed again in flat baskets, the oil from this second pressing being of lower quality than that obtained from the first. The crushed residue was used as fuel. The oil was carried home in jars, some for household consumption, the rest for sale in the market. Unlike fruits and vegetables, which were normally marketed in small quantities by women in nearby towns, olives and olive oil were marketed in the towns by men.

The fig and grape season (mawsim al-taʻzīb)

In spite of the hard work entailed, the fig and grape season was a joyful time for the peasant family. The whole family moved to the vineyards and the fig grounds, living for two or three months (between July and September) in the small rubble stone structures *(qaṣr)* built specially in the fields to accommodate the family and to store the produce. On the roof of this structure was a small canopy *m'arrash)* of sticks and tree branches to protect the family from the hot summer sun; it also provided them with an elevated spot from which to guard the vineyards and groves against thieves and wild animals, such as jackals and foxes, which are fond of grapes.

While the men were mainly responsible for marketing this summer produce, the women dried and prepared the fruit, following specific procedures for each type. The villagers followed a cyclical plan for processing and storing food to ensure that produce was available throughout the year, even out of season. Certain regions specialised in the preservation of specific foodstuffs – for example, the Ramallah area was

Men and a woman picking grapes in Artas, 1925-31.
Photo: Hilma Granqvist

Villagers posing by a watchtower and shelter *(qaṣr)* in a vineyard in Taybeh near Ramallah, 1937.
Photo: Matson Collection, Library of Congress

known for its dried figs, and both Ramallah and Hebron were known for their raisins *(zbīb)*.

Good quality white grapes were chosen for raisins. Once ripe, the fruit was carefully stripped from the bunch, leaving a little stem on each grape. The grapes were then coated with a little oil and left to dry in the sun on a surface made from flattened red soil *(misṭaḥ)*. After a few days when they became brown and wrinkled, the stems were removed and the raisins were stored in wooden boxes.

The raisin-making usually took place in September, after the Feast of the Cross. This traditional Christian feast, widely observed in Palestine, celebrated the finding of Christ's cross, and was regarded by both Christians and Muslims as an important date because it marked the hoped-for start of the rainy season after the long, hot summer.

Molasses *(dibs)* were also made from the juice of ripe grapes during the same season. This sweet light-brown treacle was an essential component of the peasant's breakfast, and was a delicious snack for children. Men made *dibs*, using abandoned wine-presses that had existed in Palestine since antiquity, and using the same methods as the ancient wine-makers to extract the juice from the grapes. Large stone slabs were laid over the grapes on the floor of the wine-press, and these were stamped on to allow the juices to flow into a series of rock-carved sloping basins. The juice was collected from the stone receptacle and boiled for several hours, skimming off the impurities, until a thick syrup was obtained.

Figs were also picked and dried at the end of the summer. There were three varieties of fig suitable for preservation – 'black' *(asmāri)*, 'blonde' *(shunnāri)* and white *(abyaḍi)*. Ripe, almost dry, figs *(thbīl)* were collected from the ground after falling from the trees, then placed on a flat soil surface *(mistah)*, or under the canopy of the field storage house *(qaṣr)*. The figs were carefully arranged so that they did not touch each other. Five days later, after they had become red and fairly dry, they were put in a special basket *(slāl 'ullayq)* woven by young men from the long-stemmed thorn bush *('ullayq)*, or the *raṭim*, a wild tree with long branches. In the home, the figs were stacked tightly in tall wooden containers *('anābir)*.

For the peasant, figs, raisins, walnuts and almonds corresponded to the sweets and cakes that city people offered their guests. A favourite village dessert consisted of dried figs dipped in *bsayseh*, a mixture of olive oil, sugar and wheat flour. Another sweet dish using dried figs was *khabīṣah*, a pudding of white dried figs, starch, and coarsely-crushed wheat.

Above: Woman from Artas taking her produce to the Bethlehem market, 1925-31.
Photo: Hilma Granqvist

Facing page: A decorative basketry tray *(sinīyyeh)* of the type used at weddings to display the trousseau. Sinjil area, north of Ramallah, 1960s.
Museum of Mankind: 1971 AS2 21 (D.92 cm)

Village Crafts

Woman making a tray or bowl from coiled basketry, highland Palestine, British Mandate period.
Photo: Matson Collection, Library of Congress

Basketry

After the wheat had been threshed, women selected the longer, unbroken stalks for basket-making, an activity reserved for winter when there was little work to be done in the fields. Women often sat around the fireplace, working their straw objects with rhythm and great artistry, and produced a colourful range of functional and luxury containers and trays.

The wheat stalks were soaked in a large copper basin *(laqan)* filled with water which made them flexible, and throughout the basket-making process the stalks were kept damp by being covered with a humid cloth. Other stems, reserved for decoration, were soaked in red, green, purple and orange dyes.

The work began by plaiting together three straw stalks, making a coil round which other stalks were bound and twisted to make a spiral. Then holes were made in the spiral with a pointed metal tool *(mikhraz)*, and straw stems were pushed through, building them up evenly and rhythmically into larger spirals. Sometimes dyed or white stems, or brown porcupine spines, were woven in to make a colourful pattern.

A variety of basketry was produced. Round trays *(ṭabaq)*, often decorated with geometric and spiral patterns, were important peasant household articles with a variety of functions. The less ornate trays *(minqaleh)* were used to cover the dough bowl or to carry the bread back from the *ṭābūn* after baking. Larger trays were placed on the floor for spreading out the food for the family meal. The most spectacular use of the tray was during the wedding when women from the bridegroom's family went singing in procession to the bride's house, carrying on their heads bridal trays *(sinīyyeh)* containing money and other presents such as clothes, sugar and coffee, all beautifully displayed on a bed of freshly cut flowers. Trays were also used as wall decorations or displayed against the smooth surface of a storage bin *(khābiyeh)*.

Other basketry objects made by women included rounded containers *(jūneh)* for bread, and *(qub'ah* and *qadaḥ)* for fruits, grain and vegetables. The *qadaḥ* was covered with animal hide to protect the contents from humidity.

Other basketry containers *(qūṭeh)* were for trinkets. One was pear-shaped with a narrow neck-opening for inserting the hand. This was often hung from its handle by a chain from the ceiling, and was used by women to store scissors, embroidery thread, keys and other tools. Another type of *qūṭeh*, consisting of a square box with a triangular top and decorated with floss silk fringes *(dhbabīḥ)*, was specially made for the bride's accessories or toiletries such as bracelets, beads, kerchiefs and kohl.

During the harvest days while working in the fields, men made corn dollies *(mushṭ)* from the wheat heads and stems. These were hung in the house as a symbol of fertility and prosperity.

Pottery

In the villages, pottery vessels were traditionally handmade by women. The potter's wheel was used only in the towns, where men were the potters, producing a different sort of functional pottery for the market. The women of the villages of Sinjil, Beitunia and Ramallah were known for their intricately decorated jars, having learned the craft from their mothers and grandmothers. They made functional, unglazed forms from local low-fired clays.

The pottery-making season started in late spring when the weather allowed a thorough drying of the vessels and when enough dried brush and branches could be collected for the

Women making water pots *(zīr)*, Beitunia near Ramallah, British Mandate period.
Photo: Matson Collection, Library of Congress

firing pit. Women potters did a great deal of strenuous work digging for and preparing the clay. They would first grind the clay rocks with heavy stone rollers, and then sift, weigh and add the correct ratio of other clay additives such as straw, sand and grog. The latter was made of powdered pottery sherds collected from nearby archaeological sites. These added materials were meant to improve the porosity and fire-resistance of the clay. The mixture was then kneaded thoroughly adding the necessary amount of water to improve its workability. At this stage, the young women in the family gave a helping hand, but once the actual forming of the pot started, the skilled potter worked alone. The work, which was done in the courtyard, proceeded in several stages: large slabs were gradually added, then the inside and outside surfaces of the vessel were smoothed with a *mashshākah*, a tool made of wood or shaped from an old pot fragment. Each time a few slab layers were added, the pot was left in the sun to dry so as to withstand the additional weight of the next layer.

At the leather-hard stage, the finished pot was coated on the outside with a light coloured slip, preparing the background for the painted decoration. The red linear motifs were painted

Right: Women making clay bowls, Ramallah, 1905.
Photo: Library of Congress

Below: On the left a decorated water jar *(jarrah)*, Sinjil, and on the right, a cooking pot *(qidreh)*.
Museum of Mankind: 1971 AS2 11 (H.33 cm); 1971 AS2 13 (W.27.5 cm)

with an iron-oxide-based pigment extracted from a reddish rock *(mighrah)* in the Ghor (the Jordan valley). Triangular shapes and hatched designs covered the whole vessel, leaving a small undercoated area just above the base. There is a strong similarity between these patterns and those found on Palestinian pots dating to the Middle Bronze Age, indicating a degree of continuity of local traditions and material culture despite the great historic changes in the region.

The finished pots were left to dry for a couple of weeks, then put in a pit filled with brush *(jalleh)* and cow dung cakes, and a fire was burnt for about two hours. Alternatively, if the pots were small, they were sometimes fired in the *ṭābūn,* the bread oven, in the courtyard. During the firing the women gathered together, singing songs expressing the hope that only a few pots would break.

The finished pots varied in size and form. The large water jar *(zīr* or *hishsheh),* which was also used to store oil, had a generously rounded belly with four handles, and was often placed at the entrance of the house for people to drink from. Small jugs *(maghāṭis)* and bowls *(zabādi)* were made for cooking and food preparation. A large two-handled cooking pot *(qidreh),* and a strainer *(miṣfāh)* were specially made for use at the fireplace. A curiously-shaped bowl on a central footstand *(miwḍah)* was made specifically for Muslims' ritual ablutions before prayers.

Weaving

Hebron and the southern region of Palestine were famed for their weaving crafts. The peasants and bedouin of these areas relied primarily on herding for their livelihood, their sheep and goats being a valuable source of meat and milk as well as wool.

The weaving season started in spring and lasted until September or October, or as long as the weather remained dry, since weaving was done mainly in the courtyard. As with most other village crafts in Palestine, weaving was the responsibility of women. The men's share in production was the shearing of the animals and the marketing of the finished product in nearby towns and villages.

After the animals had been shorn, the women washed and hand-spun the wool, using the drop-and-spin method involving a simple wooden spindle *(maghzal).* Some yarns were then coloured with dyes which were extracted from wild plants growing in Palestine. Red was made from madder, a climbing plant with yellowish flowers, or from the cochineal

Women weaving a rug *(bjād)* in Samu'ah south of Hebron, 1967.
Photo: Shelagh Weir

cactus; red-brown, yellow and blue-purple were extracted from kermes, saffron and indigo respectively.

The weaving was done on a horizontal ground loom, the treadle loom being used only by town craftsmen. It was customary to see many looms neatly stretched out on the ground, with groups of two or three women sitting weaving at one end of the loom, while onlookers sat around exchanging news and creating an atmosphere of merriment to relieve the monotony of the weavers' work.

The ground loom *(nol)* was a simple apparatus comprising two beams securely attached to the ground, between which the warp threads were stretched. The length of the article was determined by the distance between the two beams. The standard rug *(bsāṭ)* was about 4m long and 2.5m wide. The *mizwadeh* was a little shorter (3.5m), and the width was made of two joined lengths of *bsāṭ*. The loom had a fixed heddle *(minqal)* which separated the two sets of warp threads. The weaving was done by raising or lowering the alternate sets of warp threads by vigorous hand movements and with the aid of a sword beater *(minhaz)* turned on edge to hold them apart. The weft was inserted on a stick spool *(musha')*, and each woven row was tightly beaten-in with the sword beater, and a smooth metal point *(qarn)*.

Weaving required strength, technical ability and a great degree of rhythm and harmony in the body and hand movements of the weavers, who often worked in pairs or threes. Sitting on one end of the rug, their body weight keeping the warp threads in tension, they worked in unison swaying back and forth picking the thread, passing the stick spool and beating in the weft threads tightly towards them. A complete rug required a full week's work by three women.

The articles they produced were all indispensable household items. For instance, rugs *(bsāṭ, mizwadeh* or *bjād* depending on their size and colour) which had colourful thick tassels at each corner; fringed storage bags *(khurj)* for storing grain and clothes; saddle bags for donkeys, camels and horses; hammock cradles for carrying babies.

The main colours of these articles were deep crimson as background, with dark green, dark blue and white stripes. Rugs and bags provided a warm note of colour inside the often dark village home.

Bibliography

Abdulfattah K. 1983. 'The geographical distribution of the Palestinians on both sides of the 1949 armistice line', in A. Scholch (ed.), *Palestinians Over the Green Line*. London: Ithaca Press.

Abdul Jabbar, N. 1987. *Catalogue of the Palestine Folklore Museum*. Al-Bireh: Society of In'ash al-Usrah (in Arabic).

Amiry, S. 1987. *Space, Kinship and Gender: The Social Dimension of Peasant Architecture in Palestine*. Unpublished Ph.D thesis, Edinburgh University.

Baldensberger, P.J. 1913 *The Immovable East*. London: Pitman.

Canaan, T. 1932-3. 'The Palestinian Arab house: its architecture and folklore', in *Journal of the Palestine Oriental Society*, XII, 1932; XIII, 1933.

Graham-Brown, S. 1980. *Palestinians and Their Society, 1880-1946*. London: Quartet.

Grant, E. 1921. *The People of Palestine*. London: Lippincott.

Granqvist, H. 1931. *Marriage Conditions in a Palestinian Village* I. Helsinki: Societas Scientiarum Fennica.

Hasan, O. 1982. 'Folk crafts: straw weaving', in *Al-Turath wa al-Mujtama'*, 16: 65-78. Al-Bireh (in Arabic).

Kan'anah, S. 1980. 'Al-tabun' in, *At-Turath wa al-Mujtama'*, IV (13): 104-7; IV (14): 106-7; IV (15): 80-4; (16): 47-51. Al-Bireh (in Arabic).

Mason, J. and Taylor, L. 3 July, 1988. 'Village pottery: a dying tradition' in *Jordan Times*, Amman.

Mason, J. and Taylor, L. 4 July, 1988. 'Pottery reflects women's creativity', in *Jordan Times*, Amman.

Mason, J. and Taylor, L. 5 July, 1988. 'Warmth and spirit give strength to village pottery', in *Jordan Times*, Amman.

Nasir, M. 1974. 'The annual agricultural cycle of the Birzeit peasant', in *At-Turath wa al-Mujtama'*, I (1): 70-9 (in Arabic).

Palestine Folklore Committee. 1973. *Turmus'ayya: A Study of the Palestinian Cultural and Folklore Heritage*. Beirut: Palestine Research Centre (in Arabic).

Seger, K. (ed.) 1981. *Portrait of a Palestinian Village*. London: Third World Centre for Research and Publishing.

Weir, S. 1970. *Spinning and Weaving in Palestine*. London: British Museum.

Weir, S. 1976. *The Bedouin*. London: World of Islam Festival Publishing Co.

Wilson, C.T. 1906. *Peasant Life in the Holy Land*. London: Murray.